Contents

Classic Pot Roast

SERVES: 8
PREP TIME: 15 minutes, plus overnight to dry-brine
COOK TIME: 5 to 5½ hours

INGREDIENTS

- 1 (3½- to 4-pound) bottom round rump roast

- Kosher salt, for dry-brining and seasoning
- 1 tablespoon vegetable oil
- 1 onion, coarsely chopped
- 2 carrots, coarsely chopped
- 2 celery stalks, coarsely chopped
- 3 garlic cloves, coarsely chopped
- Freshly ground black pepper
- 2 tablespoons tomato paste
- 3 cups low-sodium beef broth
- 2 bay leaves

DIRECTIONS

Step 1

Dry-brine the roast overnight (see Prepping Techniques).

Step 2

The next day, remove the roast from the refrigerator and pat dry with paper towels.

Step 3

Preheat the oven to 350°F. In a large, oven-safe pot, heat the oil over medium-high heat until shimmering.

Step 4

Add the roast. Cook for 12 to 16 minutes, turning every 3 to 4 minutes, or until browned on all sides. Transfer to a plate.

Step 5

Add the onion, carrots, celery, and garlic. Cook, stirring occasionally, for 8 to 10 minutes, or until softened and browned. Season with salt and pepper.

Step 6

Add the tomato paste. Cook for 1 minute, or until bright red.

Step 7

Pour in the beef broth to deglaze: Bring to a boil, and gently scrape the bottom of the pot with a wooden spoon to loosen any browned bits.

Step 8

Add the bay leaves and put the roast back in the pot. Cover with a tight-fitting lid.

Step 9

Transfer the pot to the oven. Cook for 4½ to 5 hours, or until the beef is tender. Remove from the oven. Discard the bay leaves. Serve immediately.

Pot Roast Ragù

COOKING METHOD: stovetop
SERVES: 4
PREP TIME: 15 minutes
COOK TIME: 50 minutes

INGREDIENTS

- 1 tablespoon extra-virgin olive oil
- 1 red onion, finely diced
- 1 large carrot, finely diced
- 1 celery stalk, finely diced
- Kosher salt
- Freshly ground black pepper
- 3 garlic cloves, thinly sliced
- 3 tablespoons tomato paste
- ½ cup red wine or 1 (14-ounce) can diced tomatoes
- 3 cups whole milk
- 2 bay leaves
- 1 pound leftover Classic Pot Roast , shredded into large chunks
- 1 pound fresh pappardelle or fettuccine
- ¼ cup finely chopped fresh flat-leaf parsley
- 1 cup grated Parmigiano-Reggiano

DIRECTIONS

Step 1

In a large pot, heat the oil over medium heat until hot.

Step 2

Add the onion, carrot, and celery. Cook, stirring occasionally, for 8 to 10 minutes, or until translucent and softened. Season with salt and pepper. Add the garlic. Cook for 1 minute, or until fragrant.

Step 3

Add the tomato paste. Cook for 1 minute, or until bright red. Stir to combine. Add the wine. Cook for 2 to 3 minutes, or until evaporated.

Step 4

Add the milk, bay leaves, and leftover pot roast. Bring to a simmer. Cook, stirring occasionally to break down the meat, for 25 to 30 minutes, or until the sauce has thickened to a gravy consistency. Season with salt and pepper.

Step 5

In the last 10 to 15 minutes of cooking, bring a large pot of salted water to a boil.

Step 6

Add the pappardelle. Cook for 1 to 2 minutes, or until just shy of al dente. Strain, reserving 1 cup of cooking water.

Step 7

Discard the bay leaves. Add the pappardelle to the ragù and cook, stirring gently, for 1 minute, or until coated. Add the reserved pasta cooking water to thin the sauce, if desired. Season with salt and pepper. Remove from the heat. Top with the parsley and Parmigiano-Reggiano. Serve immediately.

Reverse-Seared London Broil

SERVES: 4
PREP TIME: 5 minutes, plus overnight to dry-brine
COOK TIME: about 1 hour
INGREDIENTS

- 1 (1½-pound) London broil
- Kosher salt, for dry-brining
- 1 tablespoon vegetable oil
- 1 tablespoon unsalted butter
- Freshly ground black pepper

DIRECTIONS

Step 1

Dry-brine the steak overnight (see Prepping Techniques).

Step 2

The next day, remove the steak from the refrigerator and pat dry with paper towels. Leave it on the wire rack set in the sheet pan.

Step 3

Preheat the oven to 225°F.

Step 4

Transfer the sheet pan to the oven. Cook for 50 to 60 minutes, or until an instant-read thermometer inserted into the side registers 115°F (for medium). Remove from the oven.

Step 5

In a large, heavy-bottomed skillet, heat the oil over high heat until shimmering.

Step 6

Add the steak. Cook for 1 minute, or until browned.

Step 7

Flip the steak, add the butter on top, and cook for 1 minute, or until browned.

Step 8

Using tongs, pick up the steak, and sear the sides for 45 seconds each. Remove from the heat. Transfer to a cutting board and sprinkle with pepper.

Step 9

Rest the steak for 5 minutes. Using a carving knife, slice very thinly across the grain.

My Steak Salad

SERVES: 4
PREP TIME: 15 minutes
COOK TIME: 45 minutes
INGREDIENTS

For the dressing
- 18 sun-dried tomatoes in extra-virgin olive oil
- Juice of 2 lemons
- 1 tablespoon chopped fresh herbs, such as thyme, parsley, or basil
- ½ cup extra-virgin olive oil (from the sun-dried tomatoes)

For the salad
- 2 cups vegetable broth or water
- 1 cup quinoa, rinsed
- 12 rainbow carrots
- 2 tablespoons neutral oil, such as canola
- 1 watermelon radish, thinly sliced
- 1½ cups apple cider vinegar
- 3 tablespoons sugar
- 1½ teaspoons Morton's or 1 tablespoon Diamond Crystal kosher salt
- 2 green cucumbers

- ¼ cup shelled, roasted, unsalted pistachios
- 1 pound cooked steak from Reverse-Seared London Broil , very thinly sliced
- 1 pound buffalo mozzarella

To make the dressing

DIRECTIONS

Step 1

In a food processor, combine the sun-dried tomatoes, lemon juice, and herbs. With the machine running, slowly stream in the olive oil until emulsified.

To make the salad

Step 2

Preheat the oven to 475°F.

Step 3

In a small pot, bring the vegetable broth to a boil.

Step 4

Add the quinoa, reduce the heat to low, and cover with a tight-fitting lid. Cook for 15 to 20 minutes, or until tender. Remove from the heat. Spread on a sheet pan in an even layer and refrigerate until cool.

Step 5

Meanwhile, cut the carrots on a bias into ¼-inch-thick slices. In a large bowl, toss the carrots and oil to combine. Transfer to a sheet pan.

Step 6

Transfer the sheet pan to the oven, and roast the carrots for 20 to 25 minutes, or until charred around the edges. Remove from the oven. Refrigerate until cool.

Step 7

Meanwhile, in another small pot, combine the watermelon radish, vinegar, sugar, and salt. Bring to a boil, then remove from the heat. Let sit for 10 minutes to pickle. Drain. Refrigerate until cool.

Step 8

Peel and seed the cucumbers. Cut them in quarters lengthwise, then into ¼-inch-thick slices.

Step 9

In a large bowl, combine the quinoa, carrots, watermelon radish, dressing, pistachios, cucumbers, and steak. Toss until everything is coated with the dressing.

Step 10

Divide among 4 plates. Tear the mozzarella, and scatter on top. Serve immediately.

Austrian Beef Salad

COOKING METHOD: stovetop
SERVES: 4
PREP TIME: 15 minutes
COOK TIME: 5 minutes
INGREDIENTS

For the dressing
- ½ cup white wine vinegar
- ½ cup pumpkin seed oil
- Kosher salt

For the salad
- ¼ cup pumpkin seeds, for garnish
- 1 (8-inch) piece daikon radish
- 1 pound cooked steak from Reverse-Seared London Broil , very thinly sliced
- 1 cup thinly sliced white onion
- 2 cups grape or cherry tomatoes, halved
- 2 cups baby watercress

To make the dressing
DIRECTIONS
Step 1
In a bowl, whisk together the vinegar and pumpkin seed oil. Season with salt.

To make the salad
Step 2
In a small pan, toast the pumpkin seeds over medium heat for 3 to 4 minutes, shaking occasionally. Remove from the heat.
Step 3
Cut the radish into rounds, about ⅛ inch thick. Layer the rounds on 4 plates. Top with the slices of steak. Drizzle some of the dressing on top.
Step 4

Scatter the onion on top and the tomatoes, watercress, and pumpkin seeds around the edges. Drizzle with the remaining dressing. Serve immediately.

Beef Pho

COOKING METHOD: stovetop
SERVES: 4
PREP TIME: 10 minutes
COOK TIME: 5 to 5½ hours

INGREDIENTS

- 2 pounds beef knuckle bones or oxtail
- 5 quarts water, plus more as needed
- 5 whole cloves
- 5 whole star anise
- 2 bunches scallions, green and white parts, cut on a bias into ½-inch lengths, divided
- 1 cinnamon stick
- 1 (2-inch) piece fresh ginger, peeled and halved lengthwise
- 1 (4-inch) piece lemongrass, halved lengthwise
- 2 tablespoons white peppercorns
- 6 tablespoons fish sauce
- 12 ounces dried rice noodles
- 8 ounces thinly sliced top round
- Hoisin sauce, for serving (optional)
- Sriracha, for serving (optional)
- Thai basil leaves, for serving (optional)
- Sliced jalapeños, for serving (optional)

DIRECTIONS

Step 1

In an 8-quart pot, combine the beef bones, water, cloves, star anise, 1 bunch of scallions, the cinnamon, ginger, lemongrass, and peppercorns. Bring to a simmer over medium-high heat. Cook for 4½ to 5 hours, or until any meat has fallen off the bones and the collagen has melted. Add water as needed to keep the pot about half full. Skim off and discard any scum that rises to the top. Strain, discarding the solids. Season with the fish sauce. Keep the soup piping hot for serving.

Step 2

Cook the noodles according to the package directions. Drain.

Step 3

Divide the soup, the noodles, and the remaining bunch of scallions among 4 bowls. Float the thin slices of top round in the soup. Serve immediately with hoisin, sriracha, basil, and jalapeños on the side (if using).

Bistro-Style Hanger Steak

COOKING METHOD: grill

SERVES: 4

PREP TIME: 5 minutes, plus overnight to dry-brine

COOK TIME: 10 minutes

INGREDIENTS

- 1 (½-inch-thick) hanger steak, about 1 pound
- Kosher salt, for dry-brining
- Vegetable oil, for coating the grill
- Freshly ground black pepper
- ½ cup Béarnaise Sauce

DIRECTIONS

Step 1

Dry-brine the steak overnight (see Prepping Techniques).

Step 2

The next day, remove the steak from the refrigerator and pat dry with paper towels.

Step 3

Prepare the grill for direct grilling at 500°F.

Step 4

Lightly coat the grill with oil.

Step 5

Put the steak on the grate. Cook for 4 to 4½ minutes per side for medium rare. Remove from the heat. Season with pepper.

Step 6

Rest the steak for 5 minutes before slicing thinly across the grain at a 45-degree angle. Serve with the sauce.

Beef Tartare

COOKING METHOD: none

SERVES: 4

PREP TIME: 20 minutes

INGREDIENTS

- 1 pound top sirloin steak
- Kosher salt
- Freshly ground black pepper
- ½ cup grated white onion
- ¼ cup Worcestershire sauce
- ¼ cup drained capers
- 4 teaspoons smooth Dijon mustard
- 4 teaspoons chopped fresh thyme
- 4 large egg yolks
- Tabasco sauce, for serving (optional)

DIRECTIONS

Step 1

Trim the steak of all fat and cut into ¼-inch dice.

Step 2

Put the steak in a large bowl. Season with plenty of salt and pepper.

Step 3

Add the onion, Worcestershire sauce, capers, mustard, and thyme. Stir to thoroughly combine.

Step 4

Divide among 4 plates, forming a thick pattylike shape with a dimple in the center.

Step 5

Add the egg yolks to the dimples.

Step 6

Serve immediately with Tabasco sauce on the side (if using).

The Bar Steak

COOKING METHOD: grill
SERVES: 4
PREP TIME: 10 minutes, plus overnight to make butter and dry-brine
COOK TIME: 10 minutes

INGREDIENTS

For the compound butter

- 8 tablespoons (1 stick) salted butter, softened

- 1 tablespoon finely chopped fresh herbs, such as thyme, parsley, basil, or dill

For the steak
- 2 (½-inch-thick) bavettes (sirloin flap steaks), about ½ pound each
- Kosher salt, for dry-brining
- 1 tablespoon vegetable oil
- Freshly ground black pepper

To make the compound butter

DIRECTIONS

Step 1

The night before serving, in a small bowl, combine the butter and herbs. Mix thoroughly with a fork. Wrap tightly in plastic wrap, roll into a log shape, and refrigerate.

To make the steak

Step 2

Dry-brine the beef overnight (see Prepping Techniques).

Step 3

The next day, remove the beef from the refrigerator and pat dry with paper towels.

Step 4

Prepare the grill for direct grilling at 500°F.

Step 5

Lightly coat the grill with oil.

Step 6

Put the steaks on the grate. Cook for 3 to 4 minutes per side for medium rare. Remove from the heat. Season with pepper.

Step 7

Rest the steaks for 5 minutes before slicing thinly across the grain at a 45-degree angle. Meanwhile, unwrap the compound butter, and cut into ¼-inch-thick medallions.

Step 8

Serve the steaks topped with the compound butter.

Reverse-Seared Top Sirloin Steak

SERVES: 4

PREP TIME: 5 minutes, plus overnight to dry-brine
COOK TIME: 40 minutes

INGREDIENTS

- 1 (1-inch-thick) top sirloin steak (about 1½ pounds)
- Kosher salt, for dry-brining
- 1 tablespoon vegetable oil
- 1 tablespoon unsalted butter
- Freshly ground black pepper
- ½ cup The Ultimate Steak Sauce

DIRECTIONS

Step 1

Dry-brine the steak overnight (see Prepping Techniques).

Step 2

The next day, remove the steak from the refrigerator and pat dry with paper towels. Leave it on the wire rack set in the sheet pan.

Step 3

Preheat the oven to 250°F.

Step 4

Transfer the sheet pan to the oven. Cook for 30 to 35 minutes, or until an instant-read thermometer inserted into the center registers 105°F for medium rare. Remove from the oven.

Step 5

In a large, heavy-bottomed skillet, heat the oil over high heat until shimmering.

Step 6

Add the steak. Cook for 1 minute, or until browned.

Step 7

Flip the steak, add the butter on top, and cook for 1 minute, or until browned.

Step 8

Using tongs, pick up the steak, and sear the sides for 45 seconds each. Remove from the heat. Transfer to a cutting board. Season with pepper.

Step 9

Rest the steak for 5 minutes. Slice across the grain and serve with the sauce.

Beef Shish Kebabs

COOKING METHOD: grill
SERVES: 4

PREP TIME: 5 minutes, plus overnight to dry-brine; 30 minutes to soak wooden skewers
COOK TIME: 15 to 20 minutes

INGREDIENTS

- 2 pounds bavette (sirloin flap steak), cut into 1-inch dice
- Kosher salt, for dry-brining
- Vegetable oil, for coating the grill
- Freshly ground black pepper
- 8 teaspoons za'atar

DIRECTIONS

Step 1

Dry-brine the steak overnight (see Prepping Techniques).

Step 2

The next day, remove the steak from the refrigerator and pat dry with paper towels.

Step 3

Soak wooden skewers for at least 30 minutes. Prepare the grill for direct grilling at 500°F.

Step 4

Lightly coat the grill with oil. Thread the steak onto the skewers.

Step 5

Put the steak on the grate. Cook for 3 to 4 minutes per side for medium. Remove from the heat. Season all over with pepper and the za'atar.

Bulgogi

COOKING METHOD: grill
SERVES: 4
PREP TIME: 10 minutes, plus at least 30 minutes to marinate
COOK TIME: 10 to 15 minutes

INGREDIENTS

- 2 pounds thinly sliced top sirloin steak or packaged presliced top sirloin
- 6 tablespoons soy sauce
- ¼ cup sugar
- 3 tablespoons water
- 2 tablespoons rice wine or mirin
- 2 tablespoons minced garlic
- 2 tablespoons sesame oil
- 2 teaspoons sesame seeds

- ¼ cup grated Korean pear or any apple
- ⅛ teaspoon freshly ground black pepper
- 3 scallions, cut into 2-inch pieces
- 1 small onion, sliced
- 1 small carrot, sliced
- Steamed white rice, for serving

DIRECTIONS

Step 1

If using packaged presliced meat, separate the slices and pat dry with paper towels.

Step 2

In a bowl, combine the soy sauce, sugar, water, rice wine, garlic, sesame oil, sesame seeds, pear, and pepper.

Step 3

Place the steak, scallions, onion, and carrot in the bowl. Toss gently to combine well. Refrigerate, and let marinate for at least 30 minutes or up to overnight. Drain.

Step 4

Prepare the grill for direct grilling at 500°F.

Step 5

Add the steak, onion, and carrot to the grate, spreading them out in a single layer as much as possible. Cook the vegetables until slightly caramelized and then remove from grill.

Step 6

Flip the steak and cook until slightly caramelized. Remove from the heat. Serve immediately with steamed white rice.

Spicy Chilled Beef and Buckwheat Noodles

COOKING METHOD: stovetop
SERVES: 6
PREP TIME: 20 minutes, plus overnight to dry-brine
COOK TIME: 10 minutes

INGREDIENTS

- 2 to 2½ pounds fresh soba noodles
- 1 Korean or brown Asian pear
- 1¼ cups hot gochujang
- 1 cup water or beef broth
- 2 tablespoons mirin

- 2 tablespoons toasted sesame oil
- 1 tablespoon rice vinegar
- 1 tablespoon soy sauce
- 1 teaspoon gochugaru (optional)
- 2 garlic cloves
- 1 cucumber, seeded and cut into thin matchsticks
- 1 Reverse-Seared Top Sirloin Steak , thinly sliced
- Baby watercress, for garnish (optional)
- Sesame seeds, for garnish (optional)

DIRECTIONS

Step 1

Cook the noodles according to the package directions. Drain and rinse with cold water until chilled.

Step 2

Grate ¼ cup of the pear. Cut the rest into thin matchsticks.

Step 3

In a food processor, combine the grated pear, gochujang, water, mirin, oil, vinegar, soy sauce, gochugaru (if using), and garlic. Process until a smooth sauce forms.

Step 4

Divide the noodles among 6 bowls. Pour an equal amount of sauce over each (about ½ cup). Arrange the pear matchsticks, cucumber, and steak on top. Garnish with the watercress (if using) and sesame seeds (if using). Mix thoroughly just before eating.

Vietnamese Shaking Beef

COOKING METHOD: stovetop
SERVES: 4
PREP TIME: 10 minutes, plus at least 30 minutes to marinate
COOK TIME: 10 minutes

INGREDIENTS

- ¼ cup fish sauce
- ½ cup water
- 2 tablespoons sugar
- 2 teaspoons toasted sesame oil
- 2 tablespoons hoisin sauce
- 2 teaspoons rice vinegar

- 1 teaspoon cornstarch
- 1 pound top sirloin steak, cut into 1-inch dice
- Freshly ground white pepper
- 3 scallions, cut into 2-inch pieces
- 2 teaspoons vegetable oil
- 1 small white onion, thinly sliced
- 2 tablespoons chopped garlic
- 2 tablespoons unsalted butter
- Lime wedges, for serving
- Steamed white rice, for serving

DIRECTIONS

Step 1

In a bowl, combine the fish sauce, water, sugar, sesame oil, hoisin sauce, and vinegar. Transfer half the mixture to another bowl, stir in the cornstarch, and reserve.

Step 2

Add the steak to the first bowl. Toss to combine. Season with pepper. Refrigerate and let marinate for at least 30 minutes or up to overnight. Drain.

Step 3

In a wok or large skillet, heat the oil over high heat until shimmering. Swirl to coat the surface.

Step 4

Add the steak, onion, and white parts of the scallions. Cook, shaking the pan occasionally, for 6 to 7 minutes, or until the steak has charred around the edges and the vegetables are crisp-tender. Season with pepper.

Step 5

Add the reserved cornstarch mixture. Cook for 10 to 15 seconds, or until the sauce is slightly thickened and the steak is thoroughly coated.

Step 6

Add the garlic. Cook for 1 minute, or until fragrant. Remove from the heat.

Step 7

Stir in the green parts of the scallions and the butter. Season with pepper. Serve immediately with lime wedges and steamed white rice.

Cumin Beef

COOKING METHOD: stovetop
SERVES: 4

PREP TIME: 10 minutes, plus 30 minutes to marinate

COOK TIME: 15 minutes

INGREDIENTS

- ¼ cup soy sauce, plus 2 tablespoons
- 2 tablespoons Chinese rice vinegar, such as Chinkiang
- 1 teaspoon cornstarch
- 1 pound top sirloin steak, thinly sliced
- 2 cups vegetable oil
- 3 garlic cloves, chopped
- 1 tablespoon cumin seeds
- 1 small white onion, thinly sliced
- 1 bell pepper, thinly sliced
- 1 serrano pepper, cut into thin rounds
- ¼ cup chopped cilantro, for garnish
- Steamed white rice, for serving

DIRECTIONS

Step 1

In a bowl, combine ¼ cup of soy sauce, the rice vinegar, and the cornstarch.

Step 2

Add the steak. Toss to combine. Refrigerate and let marinate for up to 30 minutes. Drain.

Step 3

In a wok or large skillet, heat the oil over high heat until shimmering. To test, toss in a piece of beef; it should crackle immediately. If not, continue heating the oil, and test again. Line a plate with paper towels.

Step 4

Working in batches to avoid crowding the pan, add the steak. Fry for 3 to 4 minutes per batch, or until the steak has crisped around the edges. Using a slotted spoon, transfer to the paper-towel-lined plate.

Step 5

Carefully drain off all but about 1 tablespoon of the oil.

Step 6

Add the garlic and cumin seeds. Cook, stirring frequently, for 30 seconds to 1 minute, or until the cumin is toasted (be careful not to let the garlic burn).

Step 7

Add the onion, bell pepper, and serrano pepper. Cook, stirring occasionally, for 2 to 3 minutes, or until slightly softened.

Step 8

Add the steak and the remaining 2 tablespoons of soy sauce. Cook, stirring frequently, for 30 seconds to 1 minute, or until the steak is coated with the sauce. Remove from the heat. Garnish with the cilantro. Serve immediately with steamed white rice.

Indonesian Beef Satay

COOKING METHOD: grill
SERVES: 4
PREP TIME: 5 minutes
COOK TIME: 10 minutes
INGREDIENTS

For the sauce
- 1 cup unsalted dry-roasted peanuts
- 2 tablespoons coconut palm or dark brown sugar
- ½ cup hot water
- 2 teaspoons sambal oelek (see note)
- 1 teaspoon kosher salt

For the skewers
- 2 pounds bavette (sirloin flap steak), cut into 1-inch dice
- Kosher salt, for dry-brining
- Vegetable oil, for coating the grill
- 4 teaspoons palm sugar
- ½ teaspoon ground turmeric

To make the sauce
DIRECTIONS
Step 1

In a food processor, combine the peanuts, sugar, water, sambal, and salt. Process until a chunky paste forms.

To make the skewers
Step 2

Dry-brine the steak overnight (see Prepping Techniques). The next day, remove the steak from the refrigerator and pat dry with paper towels.

Step 3

Soak wooden skewers in water for at least 30 minutes. Prepare the grill for direct grilling at 500°F.

Step 4

Lightly coat the grill with oil. In a bowl, toss the steak with the sugar and turmeric. Thread onto the skewers.

Step 5

Put the steak on the grate and close the lid. Cook for 3 to 4 minutes per side for medium. Remove from the heat. Serve immediately with the peanut sauce.

Reverse-Seared New York Strip

SERVES: 4
PREP TIME: 5 minutes, plus overnight to dry-brine
COOK TIME: 40 to 50 minutes
INGREDIENTS

- 2 (1½-inch-thick) New York strip steaks, about 1 pound each

- Kosher salt, for dry-brining

- 2 tablespoons vegetable oil

- 2 tablespoons unsalted butter

- Freshly ground black pepper

DIRECTIONS

Step 1

Dry-brine the steaks overnight (see Prepping Techniques).

Step 2

The next day, remove the steaks from the refrigerator and pat dry with paper towels. Leave on the wire rack set in the sheet pan.

Step 3

Preheat the oven to 250°F.

Step 4

Transfer the sheet pan to the oven. Cook for 35 to 45 minutes, or until an instant-read thermometer inserted into the center registers 105°F for medium rare. Remove from the oven.

Step 5

In a large, heavy-bottomed skillet, heat the oil over high heat until shimmering.

Step 6

Add the steaks. Cook for 1 minute, or until browned.

Step 7

Flip the steaks, add the butter on top, and cook for 1 minute, or until browned.

Step 8

Using tongs, pick up the steaks, and sear the sides for 45 seconds each. Remove from the heat. Transfer to a cutting board. Season with pepper.

Step 9

Rest the steaks for 5 minutes. Slice across the grain and serve.

The Midnight Steak Sandwich

COOKING METHOD: none
SERVES: 4
PREP TIME: 20 minutes

INGREDIENTS

- 2 tablespoons harissa
- ½ cup Aioli
- 4 French rolls or hoagie rolls, halved and lightly toasted
- 1 Reverse-Seared New York Strip , cut on a bias into ⅛-inch-thick slices
- 1 tablespoon sumac
- 1 large cucumber, shaved lengthwise on a mandoline
- 16 ripe tomato slices, preferably heirloom
- Sliced red onion, for serving
- 1 batch Perfect French Fries

DIRECTIONS

Step 1

In a small bowl, stir together the harissa and aioli. Slather onto the cut sides of the rolls.

Step 2

In a medium bowl, toss the steak with the sumac. Layer onto the rolls.

Step 3

Top the steak with the cucumber, tomato, as much red onion as you'd like, as many French fries as you can cram in, and the tops of the rolls. Press down on the rolls to sandwich everything together, then slice in half. Serve immediately.

Grilled T-Bone Steak

COOKING METHOD: grill

SERVES: 2

PREP TIME: 5 minutes, plus overnight to dry-brine

COOK TIME: varies

INGREDIENTS

- 1 (1½-inch-thick) T-bone steak, about 1¼ pounds
- Kosher salt, for dry-brining
- Vegetable oil, for coating the grill
- Freshly ground black pepper

DIRECTIONS

Step 1

Dry-brine the steak overnight (see Prepping Techniques).

Step 2

The next day, remove the steak from the refrigerator and pat dry with paper towels.

Step 3

Prepare the grill with a dual-zone fire: If using a charcoal grill, light the coals with a chimney starter, and pile them up on one side of the fire box beneath the grates, leaving the other side empty. Replace the grates, close the lid, and do your best to achieve a temperature of about 500°F on the side with the coals. (Placing a grill thermometer on the grate above the coals will help you gauge this most accurately.) If using a gas grill, set the burners on high on one side of the grill and on the lowest setting on the other.

Step 4

Lightly coat the grill with oil.

Step 5

Place the steak on the grate with the tenderloin over the cooler side and close the lid. Cook, flipping halfway through, until an instant-read thermometer inserted into the tenderloin without touching the bone registers 120°F. (When flipping the steak, make sure that the tenderloin remains on the cooler side.) Remove from the heat. Season with pepper.

Step 6

Rest the steak for 5 minutes. Slice across the grain. Serve immediately.

Bistecca alla Fiorentina

COOKING METHOD: grill

SERVES: 8

PREP TIME: 5 minutes, plus overnight to dry-brine

COOK TIME: varies

INGREDIENTS

- 1 (2-inch-thick) porterhouse steak, about 2 pounds
- Kosher salt, for dry-brining
- Vegetable oil, for coating the grill
- Freshly ground black pepper
- Freshly squeezed lemon juice, for serving
- Extra-virgin olive oil, for serving
- Chopped fresh rosemary, for serving

DIRECTIONS

Step 1

Dry-brine the steak overnight (see Prepping Techniques).

Step 2

The next day, remove the steak from the refrigerator and pat dry with paper towels.

Step 3

Prepare the grill with a dual-zone fire: If using a charcoal grill, light the coals with a chimney starter, and pile them up on one side of the fire box beneath the grates, leaving the other side empty. Replace the grates, close the lid, and do your best to achieve a temperature of about 500°F on the side with the coals. (Placing a grill thermometer on the grate above the coals will help you gauge this most accurately.) If using a gas grill, set the burners on high on one side of the grill and on the lowest setting on the other.

Step 4

Lightly coat the grill with vegetable oil.

Step 5

Place the steak on the grate with the tenderloin over the cooler side and close the lid. Cook, flipping halfway through, until an instant-read thermometer inserted into the tenderloin without touching the bone registers 120°F. (When flipping the steak, make sure that the tenderloin remains on the cooler side.) Remove from the heat. Season with pepper. Top with the lemon juice, olive oil, and rosemary.

Step 6

Rest the steak for 15 minutes. Slice across the grain. Serve immediately.

Beef Carpaccio

COOKING METHOD: none

SERVES: 4

PREP TIME: 1 hour

INGREDIENTS

- 8 ounces beef tenderloin
- Kosher salt
- Freshly ground black pepper
- 2 cups wild arugula
- ½ cup shaved Parmigiano-Reggiano
- 2 tablespoons nonpareil capers, drained
- 2 tablespoons extra-virgin olive oil
- Aged balsamic vinegar, for drizzling

DIRECTIONS

Step 1

Wrap the beef tightly in plastic wrap, and freeze for about 50 minutes, or until firm.

Step 2

Remove the plastic wrap. Using a carving knife and long smooth strokes, cut the beef into roughly ⅛-inch-thick slices (it's okay if they're a little thicker).

Step 3

Place the beef between 2 sheets of wax paper. Using the smooth side of a meat mallet, pound the beef until it's paper-thin.

Step 4

Divide the beef among 4 plates without overlapping the slices. Season with salt and pepper.

Step 5

Scatter the arugula, Parmigiano-Reggiano, and capers on top.

Step 6

Drizzle with the oil and vinegar. Serve immediately.

Filet Mignon with Bordelaise Sauce

SERVES: 2
PREP TIME: 5 minutes, plus overnight to dry-brine
COOK TIME: 30 minutes

INGREDIENTS

- 2 (1-inch-thick) filets mignons, about 12 ounces total
- Kosher salt, for dry-brining
- 2 teaspoons vegetable oil
- 1 tablespoon unsalted butter

- Freshly ground black pepper
- ¼ cup Bordelaise Sauce

DIRECTIONS

Step 1

Dry-brine the steaks overnight (see Prepping Techniques).

Step 2

The next day, remove the steaks from the refrigerator and pat dry with paper towels. Leave them on the wire rack set in the sheet pan.

Step 3

Preheat the oven to 250°F.

Step 4

Transfer the sheet pan to the oven. Cook for 20 to 25 minutes, or until an instant-read thermometer inserted into the center registers 105°F for medium rare. Remove from the oven.

Step 5

In a large, heavy-bottomed skillet, heat the oil over high heat until shimmering.

Step 6

Add the steaks. Cook for 1 minute, or until browned.

Step 7

Flip the steaks, add the butter on top of each, and cook for 1 minute, or until browned.

Step 8

Using tongs, pick up the steaks, and sear the sides for 45 seconds each. Remove from the heat. Transfer to a cutting board. Season with pepper.

Step 9

Rest the steaks for 5 minutes. Serve with the sauce.

Chateaubriand for Two

SERVES: 2
PREP TIME: 5 minutes, plus overnight to dry-brine
COOK TIME: 40 minutes

INGREDIENTS
- 1 (10-ounce) chateaubriand (beef tenderloin roast)
- Kosher salt, for dry-brining
- 1 tablespoon vegetable oil
- Freshly ground black pepper
- 1 cup Chateaubriand Sauce

DIRECTIONS

Step 1

Dry-brine the roast overnight (see Prepping Techniques).

Step 2

The next day, remove the roast from the refrigerator and pat dry with paper towels. Leave it on the wire rack set in the sheet pan.

Step 3

Preheat the oven to 250°F.

Step 4

Transfer the sheet pan to the oven. Cook for 30 to 35 minutes, or until an instant-read thermometer inserted into the center registers 100°F for medium rare. Remove from the oven.

Step 5

In a large, heavy-bottomed skillet, heat the oil over high heat until shimmering.

Step 6

Add the roast. Cook for 1 minute on each side, using tongs as needed to hold it in place, or until browned all over. Remove from the heat. Season with pepper.

Step 7

Rest the roast for 5 minutes. Slice across the grain into medallions. Serve with the sauce.

Steak Diane

COOKING METHOD: stovetop
SERVES: 4
PREP TIME: 10 minutes
COOK TIME: 25 minutes

INGREDIENTS

- 1½ pounds filet mignon (beef tenderloin medallions)
- Kosher salt
- ½ cup all-purpose flour
- 1 tablespoon vegetable oil
- 2 tablespoons unsalted butter, divided
- Freshly ground black pepper
- 4 ounces sliced white mushrooms
- 1 shallot, minced
- ¼ cup cognac
- ¼ cup veal demi-glace

- ¼ cup heavy cream
- 1 tablespoon Dijon mustard
- 2 teaspoons Worcestershire sauce

DIRECTIONS

Step 1

Place the beef between 2 sheets of wax paper. Using the smooth side of a meat mallet, pound the beef until it is ¼ inch thick. Pat dry with paper towels. Season with salt.

Step 2

Put the flour on a plate. Coat both sides of the beef in flour, shaking off any excess.

Step 3

In a large skillet, heat the oil and 1 tablespoon of butter over high heat until the butter has melted.

Step 4

Add the beef. Cook for 2 to 3 minutes for medium rare, or until golden brown. Season with pepper.

Step 5

Flip the beef, and cook for 2 to 3 minutes, or until golden brown. Season with pepper. Transfer to a plate.

Step 6

In the same pan you used to cook the beef, melt the remaining 1 tablespoon of butter over medium-high heat.

Step 7

Add the mushrooms. Cook for 4 to 5 minutes, or until lightly browned.

Step 8

Reduce the heat to medium-low. Add the shallot. Cook for 2 to 3 minutes, or until softened.

Step 9

Off the heat, pour in the cognac. Increase the heat to high, put the pan back on the burner, and carefully tip it just enough to ignite the cognac. Cook until nearly evaporated, scraping up any brown bits from the bottom of the pan.

Step 10

Stir in the demi-glace, heavy cream, mustard, and Worcestershire sauce. Season with salt and pepper. Heat through for 1 minute, or until all the flavors have combined. Remove from the heat. Serve immediately, spooned over the beef.

Japanese Miso-Marinated Beef

COOKING METHOD: oven, grill
SERVES: 4

PREP TIME: 5 minutes, plus overnight to dry-brine

COOK TIME: 40 to 50 minutes

INGREDIENTS

- 2 (1½-inch-thick) New York strip steaks, about 1 pound each, lightly scored with a knife
- Kosher salt, for dry-brining
- ¼ cup mirin
- 2 tablespoons water
- 2 tablespoons sugar
- 2 tablespoons Japanese red miso
- 2 teaspoons toasted sesame oil
- Vegetable oil, for coating the grill
- Freshly ground black pepper
- Steamed white rice, for serving

DIRECTIONS

Step 1

Dry-brine the steaks overnight (see Prepping Techniques).

Step 2

The next day, remove the steaks from the refrigerator.

Step 3

In a bowl, whisk together the mirin, water, sugar, miso, and sesame oil to make a glaze. Pour off half into a small container, and reserve. Add the steaks to the bowl, and coat well. Place back on the wire rack set in a sheet pan.

Step 4

Preheat the oven to 250°F.

Step 5

Transfer the sheet pan to the oven. Cook for 35 to 45 minutes, or until an instant-read thermometer inserted into the center registers 105°F for medium rare. Remove from the oven.

Step 6

Prepare a grill for direct grilling at 500°F. Lightly coat the grate with vegetable oil.

Step 7

Put the steaks on the grate. Cook for 2 minutes, or until char marks appear.

Step 8

Flip the steaks. Cook for 2 minutes, or until char marks appear.

Step 9

Using tongs, pick up the steaks, and sear the sides for 45 seconds each. Remove from the heat. Transfer to a cutting board. Season with pepper.

Step 10

Rest the steaks for 5 minutes. Slice across the grain. Brush with the reserved glaze. Serve with steamed rice.

Reverse-Seared Rib Eye Steak

SERVES: 4

PREP TIME: 5 minutes, plus overnight to dry-brine

COOK TIME: 50 minutes to 1 hour

INGREDIENTS

- 2 (1½-inch-thick) bone-in rib eye steaks, about 2⅔ pounds total
- Kosher salt, for dry-brining
- 2 tablespoons vegetable oil
- 2 tablespoons unsalted butter
- Freshly ground black pepper

DIRECTIONS

Step 1

Dry-brine the steaks overnight (see Prepping Techniques).

Step 2

The next day, remove the steaks from the refrigerator and pat dry with paper towels. Leave them on the wire rack set in the sheet pan.

Step 3

Preheat the oven to 250°F.

Step 4

Transfer the sheet pan to the oven. Cook for 45 to 55 minutes, or until an instant-read thermometer inserted into the center registers 105°F for medium rare. Remove from the oven.

Step 5

In a large, heavy-bottomed skillet, heat the oil over high heat until shimmering.

Step 6

Add the steaks. Cook for 1 minute, or until browned.

Step 7

Flip the steaks, add the butter on top, and cook for 1 minute, or until browned.

Step 8

Using tongs, pick up the steaks, and sear the sides for 45 seconds each. Remove from the heat. Transfer to a cutting board. Season with pepper.

Step 9

Rest the steaks for 5 minutes. Slice across the grain, and serve immediately.

Steak Frites

SERVES: 4

PREP TIME: 5 minutes, plus overnight to dry-brine

COOK TIME: 50 minutes to 1 hour

INGREDIENTS

- 2 (1½-inch-thick) bone-in rib eye steaks, about 2⅔ pounds
- Kosher salt, for dry-brining
- 2 tablespoons vegetable oil
- 2 tablespoons unsalted butter
- Freshly ground black pepper
- 1 batch Perfect French Fries

DIRECTIONS

Step 1

Dry-brine the steaks overnight (see Prepping Techniques).

Step 2

The next day, remove the steaks from the refrigerator and pat dry with paper towels. Leave them on the wire rack set in the sheet pan.

Step 3

Preheat the oven to 250°F.

Step 4

Transfer the sheet pan to the oven. Cook for 45 to 55 minutes, or until an instant-read thermometer inserted into the center registers 105°F for medium rare. Remove from the oven.

Step 5

In a large, heavy-bottomed skillet, heat the oil over high heat until shimmering.

Step 6

Add the steaks. Cook for 1 minute, or until browned.

Step 7

Flip the steaks, add the butter on top, and cook for 1 minute, or until browned.

Step 8

Using tongs, pick up the steaks, and sear the sides for 45 seconds each. Remove from the heat. Transfer to a cutting board. Season with pepper.

Step 9

Rest the steaks for 5 minutes. Slice across the grain and serve with the French fries.

Steak and Eggs

SERVES: 4
PREP TIME: 5 minutes, plus overnight to dry-brine
COOK TIME: 1 hour to 1 hour 10 minutes
INGREDIENTS

For the steak
- 2 (1½-inch-thick) bone-in rib eye steaks, about 2⅔ pounds
- Kosher salt, for dry-brining
- 2 tablespoons vegetable oil
- 2 tablespoons unsalted butter, plus more as needed
- Freshly ground black pepper

For the eggs
- 8 large eggs

To make the steak
DIRECTIONS
Step 1
Dry-brine the steak overnight (see Prepping Techniques).
Step 2
The next day, remove the steaks from the refrigerator and pat dry with paper towels. Leave them on the wire rack set in the sheet pan.
Step 3
Preheat the oven to 250°F.
Step 4
Transfer the sheet pan to the oven. Cook for 45 to 55 minutes, or until an instant-read thermometer inserted into the center registers 105°F for medium rare. Remove from the oven.
Step 5
In a large, heavy-bottomed skillet, heat the oil over high heat until shimmering.
Step 6
Add the steaks. Cook for 1 minute, or until browned.
Step 7

Flip the steaks, add the butter on top, and cook for 1 minute, or until browned.

Step 8

Using tongs, pick up the steaks, and sear the sides for 45 seconds each. Remove from the heat. Transfer to a cutting board. Season with pepper.

Step 9

Rest the steaks for 5 minutes. Slice across the grain.

To make the eggs

Step 10

In the same pan used to sear the steaks, cook the eggs in your desired style, adding more butter as needed.

Step 11

Serve the steaks with the eggs.

Steak au Poivre

SERVES: 4

PREP TIME: 5 minutes, plus overnight to dry-brine

COOK TIME: 25 minutes

INGREDIENTS

For the steaks

- 2 (1½-inch-thick) bone-in rib eye steaks, about 2⅔ pounds
- Kosher salt, for dry-brining
- 2 tablespoons vegetable oil
- 2 tablespoons unsalted butter
- Freshly ground black pepper

For the sauce

- 1 shallot, minced
- 2 tablespoons cognac
- ½ cup heavy cream
- 2 tablespoons green peppercorns in brine, drained
- 1 bay leaf
- Kosher salt

- Freshly ground black pepper

To make the steaks

DIRECTIONS

Step 1

Dry-brine the steaks overnight (see Prepping Techniques).

Step 2

The next day, remove the steak from the refrigerator and pat dry with paper towels.

Step 3

Preheat the oven to 350°F.

Step 4

In a large, heavy-bottomed, oven-safe skillet, heat the oil over high heat until shimmering.

Step 5

Add the steaks. Cook for 2 minutes, or until browned.

Step 6

Flip the steaks, add 1 tablespoon of butter on top of each steak, and cook for 2 minutes, or until browned.

Step 7

Using tongs, pick up the steaks, and sear the sides for 45 seconds each. Remove from the heat.

Step 8

Transfer the pan to the oven. Cook for 10 to 12 minutes, or until an instant-read thermometer inserted into the center registers 115°F for medium rare. Remove from the oven.

Step 9

Transfer the steaks to a cutting board. Season generously with black pepper.

To make the sauce

Step 10

In the same pan used to cook the steak, cook the shallot over medium-low heat for 3 to 4 minutes, or until softened but not taking on color.

Step 11

Off the heat, pour in the cognac. Increase the heat to high, put the pan back on the burner, and carefully tip it just enough to ignite the cognac. Cook until the cognac is nearly evaporated, scraping up any brown bits from the bottom of the pan.

Step 12

Reduce the heat to medium. Add the heavy cream, green peppercorns, and bay leaf. Cook for 3 to 4 minutes, or just until the sauce coats the back of a spoon. Season with salt. Remove from the heat. Season generously with black pepper.

Step 13

Slice the steak the across the grain and serve immediately with the sauce.

Prime Rib Fit for a Party

SERVES: 8 to 12

PREP TIME: 5 minutes, plus overnight to dry-brine

COOK TIME: 2½ to 3 hours

INGREDIENTS

- 1 (6- to 7-pound) three-bone prime rib or standing rib roast

- Kosher salt, for dry-brining

- 1 tablespoon vegetable oil

- Freshly ground black pepper

- 1 batch Horseradish Sauce

DIRECTIONS

Step 1

Dry-brine the roast overnight (see Prepping Techniques).

Step 2

The next day, remove the roast from the refrigerator and pat dry with paper towels.

Step 3

Preheat the oven to 250°F.

Step 4

Place the roast in a roasting pan, making sure the roast is bone-side up. Transfer the roasting pan to the oven, with the bone facing the back of the oven. Roast for 2½ to 3 hours, or until an instant-read thermometer inserted into the center registers 100°F for rare. Remove from the oven.

Step 5

In a large, heavy-bottomed skillet, heat the oil over high heat until shimmering.

Step 6

Add the roast. Cook for 1 minute on each side, using tongs (or barbecue gloves) as needed to hold it in place, or until browned all over. Remove from the heat and season with pepper. Reserve any juices from the skillet and roasting pan for serving.

Step 7

Rest the roast for 30 minutes. Carve off the bone, then slice thinly crosswise. Serve immediately with the horseradish sauce.

Beef Stroganoff

COOKING METHOD: stovetop
SERVES: 6
PREP TIME: 10 minutes
COOK TIME: 40 to 45 minutes

INGREDIENTS

- 1 (1-pound) boneless rib eye steak, cut into ¼-inch-thick slices
- Kosher salt
- 6 tablespoons vegetable oil, divided
- Freshly ground black pepper
- 1 pound mixed mushrooms, such as cremini, oyster, or shiitake, sliced
- 1 large onion, finely chopped
- 2 cups beef broth
- 1½ cups heavy cream
- 8 ounces egg noodles
- 2 tablespoons Dijon mustard
- 8 ounces sour cream
- 6 tablespoons chopped fresh dill

DIRECTIONS

Step 1

Pat the steak dry. Season with salt.

Step 2

In a large, heavy-bottomed skillet, heat 1 tablespoon of oil over high heat until shimmering.

Step 3

Add the steak. Cook for 5 to 6 minutes on each side, or until browned all over. Using a slotted spoon, transfer to a plate. Season with pepper.

Step 4

Reduce the heat to medium-high. Working in batches, add the remaining 5 tablespoons of oil and the mushrooms to the same pan. Cook for 7 to 8 minutes per batch, or until browned. Using a slotted spoon, transfer to a plate. Season with salt and pepper.

Step 5

Reduce the heat to medium. Add the onion. Cook for 5 to 6 minutes, or until softened and translucent.

Step 6

Add the beef broth, heavy cream, and egg noodles. Bring to a simmer. Season with salt and pepper. Cook, stirring occasionally, for 8 to 9 minutes, or until the noodles are al dente, or tender but with a slight bite.

Step 7

Add the mushrooms and steak back to the pan. Cook for 1 minute, or until heated through. Remove from the heat.

Step 8

Stir in the mustard and sour cream until fully incorporated.

Step 9

Top with the dill. Serve immediately.

Sukiyaki

COOKING METHOD: stovetop

SERVES: 4

PREP TIME: 10 minutes

COOK TIME: 25 to 35 minutes

INGREDIENTS

- 2 tablespoons unsalted butter
- 1 large onion, finely chopped
- 2 cups water
- 1 cup beef broth
- ½ cup soy sauce
- ½ cup sugar
- ¼ cup mirin
- 1 carrot, cut into matchsticks
- 6 ounces extra-firm tofu, diced
- 7 ounces fresh udon noodles
- 7 ounces glass noodles
- 3½ ounces beech mushrooms (or enoki or shiitake)
- 4 cups chopped napa cabbage
- 1 teaspoon cornstarch
- 1 pound boneless rib eye steak, thinly sliced
- 2 scallions, green and white parts, cut on a bias into 1-inch pieces
- Steamed white rice, for serving

DIRECTIONS

Step 1

In a large pot, melt the butter over medium heat.

Step 2

Add the onion. Cook for 8 to 10 minutes, or until golden brown.

Step 3

Add the water, beef broth, soy sauce, sugar, and mirin. Bring to a boil, then reduce the heat to a simmer.

Step 4

Add the carrot and tofu. Cook for 2 to 3 minutes, or until the carrot is crisp-tender.

Step 5

Add the udon noodles and glass noodles. Cook for 2 to 3 minutes, or until the udon is nearly al dente.

Step 6

Add the mushrooms. Cook for 1 to 2 minutes, or until still a bit firm.

Step 7

Add the cabbage. Cook for 1 to 2 minutes, or until slightly wilted.

Step 8

Add the cornstarch. Bring to a boil. Reduce the heat to medium. Simmer for 3 to 4 minutes, or until slightly thickened.

Step 9

Add the steak and scallions. Cook for 2 to 3 minutes, or until the steak is cooked through and thoroughly coated with the sauce. Remove from the heat. Serve with steamed white rice.

Brothless Steak Ramen

COOKING METHOD: stovetop
SERVES: 4
PREP TIME: 10 minutes
COOK TIME: 20 to 25 minutes

INGREDIENTS

- 2 (10-ounce) packages fresh ramen noodles
- 2 tablespoons vegetable oil
- 10 ounces shiitake mushrooms, stemmed and quartered
- 2 tablespoons unsalted butter
- 1 large red onion, finely diced
- ¼ cup red miso

- ¼ cup soy sauce
- 1 cup beef broth
- ½ cup mirin
- 2 tablespoons sugar
- 2 tablespoons rice vinegar
- ¼ teaspoon cornstarch
- 1 Reverse-Seared Rib Eye Steak , cut into 1-inch dice
- 4 cups baby watercress or arugula, for garnish
- 2 tablespoons sesame seeds

DIRECTIONS

Step 1

Cook the noodles according to the package directions. Drain.

Step 2

In a large skillet, heat the oil over high heat.

Step 3

Add the mushrooms. Cook for 4 to 6 minutes, or until softened and slightly charred. Transfer to a plate.

Step 4

In the same pan, melt the butter over medium heat.

Step 5

Add the onion. Cook for 5 to 6 minutes, or until softened.

Step 6

Meanwhile, in a bowl, whisk together the miso, soy sauce, beef broth, mirin, sugar, vinegar, and cornstarch until the miso has dissolved.

Step 7

Add the miso mixture to the pan. Bring to a boil. Reduce the heat to a simmer. Cook for 1 to 2 minutes, or until the flavors meld.

Step 8

Add the noodles, mushrooms, and beef. Cook for 1 minute, or until everything is heated through and the noodles are thoroughly coated. Remove from the heat. Divide among 4 wide bowls. Garnish with the greens and sesame seeds. Serve immediately.

Smoked Beef Ribs

COOKING METHOD: smoker
SERVES: 6

PREP TIME: 1 hour, plus overnight to dry-brine
COOK TIME: 5 to 6 hours, plus resting 1 hour

INGREDIENTS

- 1 (3- to 5-pound) rack beef back ribs
- Kosher salt, for dry-brining
- 2 tablespoons freshly ground black pepper
- Vegetable oil

DIRECTIONS

Step 1

Trim any hanging pieces of fat off the ribs.

Step 2

Dry-brine the beef back ribs overnight (see Prepping Techniques).

Step 3

The next day, remove the ribs from the refrigerator. Season with the pepper. Soak wood chips or chunks (preferably oak or pecan, but any nonresinous hardwood will do) in water for at least 15 minutes. Preheat the smoker to 275°F, and add the soaked wood, following the manufacturer's instructions.

Step 4

Place the ribs on oiled grates, meat-side up. Close the cooking compartment, and smoke for 5 to 6 hours, or until an instant-read thermometer inserted without touching the bone reads 200°F. Add wood and fuel, as necessary, to maintain smoke and temperature. Avoid opening the lid unnecessarily; this will prolong the cook time significantly.

Step 5

Allow the ribs to rest for 60 minutes before serving.

Classic Beef Meatballs

COOKING METHOD: stovetop
SERVES: 4
PREP TIME: 25 minutes
COOK TIME: 25 to 30 minutes

INGREDIENTS

- 1½ pounds freshly ground chuck
- 1 large egg
- 4 garlic cloves, finely chopped
- ¾ cup finely diced red onions
- ½ cup plain bread crumbs

- 1 tablespoon dried oregano
- Kosher salt
- Freshly ground black pepper
- 1 teaspoon extra-virgin olive oil
- 3½ cups tomato sauce
- ½ cup grated Parmigiano-Reggiano cheese

DIRECTIONS

Step 1

In a large bowl, combine the ground beef, egg, garlic, onions, bread crumbs, and oregano. Season generously with salt and pepper. Mix until just incorporated; form into 1-inch meatballs.

Step 2

Heat the oil in a large pot over medium heat. Once the oil is hot, working in batches if necessary, add the meatballs in a single layer. Cook, turning occasionally, for 16 to 20 minutes, or until lightly browned on all sides.

Step 3

Add the tomato sauce. Cover the pot with a tight-fitting lid. Cook for 10 minutes, or until the flavors meld. Remove from the heat, top with the cheese, and serve immediately.

My Perfect Burger

COOKING METHOD: stovetop, grill
SERVES: 4
PREP TIME: 10 minutes
COOK TIME: 20 to 25 minutes

INGREDIENTS

- 8 bacon slices
- 8 ounces cremini mushrooms, sliced
- Kosher salt
- Freshly ground black pepper
- 2 pounds freshly ground chuck
- 4 sharp Cheddar slices
- 4 brioche buns, split
- ½ cup Aioli
- 4 tomato slices, preferably heirloom
- Sliced red onion, for serving
- Iceberg lettuce, for serving

DIRECTIONS

Step 1

Prepare the grill for direct grilling at 500°F. On the stovetop, heat a 10-inch skillet over medium heat.

Step 2

Put the bacon in the skillet. Cook, flipping once, for 3 to 5 minutes, or until browned and crispy around the edges. Remove from the heat. Transfer to a plate.

Step 3

Increase the heat to high. Add the mushrooms to the rendered fat. Cook, stirring once, for 7 to 9 minutes, or until browned. Remove from the heat and transfer to a plate. Season with salt and pepper.

Step 4

Meanwhile, in a large bowl, season the beef with pepper and 4 teaspoons of salt. Using your hands, mix until just incorporated; form into 4 (1-inch-thick) patties with a slight dimple in the center.

Step 5

On the grill, put the patties on the grate, and close the lid. Cook for 4 to 5 minutes per side for medium, or until an instant-read thermometer inserted into the center registers 135°F. In the last minute of cooking, top the patties with the cheese to melt, and place the buns, cut-side down, on the grate to toast. Remove from the heat.

Step 6

Spread the aioli on the buns, and assemble the burgers with the bacon, mushrooms, tomato, onion, and lettuce. Serve immediately.

salt and pepper. Serve immediately over steamed white rice or a baguette.

Indonesian Beef Rendang

COOKING METHOD: stovetop

SERVES: 6

PREP TIME: 10 minutes, plus overnight to dry-brine

COOK TIME: 2¾ to 3¼ hours

INGREDIENTS

- 2 pounds boneless beef chuck roast, cut into 1-inch pieces

- Kosher salt, for dry-brining

- 2 tablespoons vegetable oil

- 10 shallots, chopped

- 6 garlic cloves, chopped

- 4 Thai red chiles, stemmed and chopped (10 to 12 for the full experience)

- 1 lemongrass stalk, tough ends and outer layers removed, chopped (see Prep Ahead)
- ½ teaspoon ground turmeric
- 2 turmeric leaves (optional)
- 2 teaspoons finely chopped fresh galangal (or double the amount of fresh ginger)
- 2 teaspoons finely chopped fresh ginger
- 4 (13½-ounce) cans coconut milk
- Steamed white rice, for serving

DIRECTIONS

Step 1

Dry-brine the beef overnight (see Prepping Techniques).

Step 2

The next day, remove the beef from the refrigerator and pat dry with paper towels.

Step 3

In a large pot, heat the oil over low heat.

Step 4

In a mortar and pestle or food processor, combine the shallots, garlic, chiles, lemongrass, turmeric, turmeric leaves (if using), galangal, and ginger. Pound or pulse into a coarse paste. Transfer to the large pot. Sweat, stirring occasionally, for 30 minutes, or until the heat of the chiles is tempered and the flavors meld.

Step 5

Add the coconut milk. Increase the heat to medium-high. Bring to a vigorous simmer, but do not boil or the coconut milk will separate.

Step 6

Add the beef. Reduce the heat to medium. Cook, stirring occasionally, for 2 to 2½ hours, or until the fat from the coconut milk floats to the top and the beef is coated with gravy the color of milk chocolate. Reduce the heat as needed to maintain a gentle simmer. Remove from the heat.

Step 7

Using a slotted spoon, transfer the beef to a serving dish, leaving any excess fat behind. Serve with plenty of steamed rice.

Fiery Southern Thai Curry Beef

COOKING METHOD: stovetop
SERVES: 4
PREP TIME: 15 minutes, plus at least 30 minutes to marinate
COOK TIME: 15 minutes
INGREDIENTS

- 10 makrut lime leaves, divided, center stems removed (or 5 teaspoons grated lime zest)
- 1 (1-inch) piece fresh ginger, peeled and sliced
- 1 shallot, chopped
- 1 lemongrass stalk, tough ends and outer leaves discarded, minced
- 1 tablespoon Thai red chiles, stemmed and chopped (¼ cup for spicy)
- Juice of 1 lime
- 1 tablespoon fish sauce
- 1 tablespoon sugar
- 1 teaspoon shrimp paste
- 2 ounces fresh turmeric, peeled and chopped (or ¼ teaspoon ground turmeric)
- 1 pound chuck tender, thinly sliced
- 1 tablespoon vegetable oil
- ¼ cup chopped cilantro, for garnish
- Steamed white rice, for serving

DIRECTIONS

Step 1

Using a mortar and pestle, pound 5 of the lime leaves and the ginger, shallot, lemongrass, chiles, lime juice, fish sauce, sugar, shrimp paste, and turmeric together. (You can also use a food processor and pulse everything into a coarse paste; just chop the tough ingredients like ginger and lemongrass more finely before processing.) Transfer to a medium bowl.

Step 2

Very thinly slice the remaining 5 lime leaves and set aside.

Step 3

Add the steak to the bowl with the curry paste. Toss to combine. Refrigerate, and let marinate for at least 30 minutes or up to overnight.

Step 4

Heat a wok or large skillet until smoking hot.

Step 5

Pour in the oil and swirl to coat the surface.

Step 6

Add the beef. Cook, shaking the pan once any liquid has evaporated, for 12 to 14 minutes, or until the beef has charred around the edges.

Step 7

Add the reserved 5 lime leaves. Cook for 10 to 15 seconds, or until fragrant. Remove from the heat.

Step 8

Garnish with the cilantro. Serve with steamed white rice.

Red Wine–Braised Short Ribs

SERVES: 4

PREP TIME: 10 minutes, plus overnight to dry-brine

COOK TIME: 3¼ to 4 hours

INGREDIENTS

- 2½ to 3 pounds bone-in short ribs
- Kosher salt, for dry-brining and seasoning
- 1 tablespoon vegetable oil
- 1 onion, coarsely chopped
- 1 carrot, coarsely chopped
- 1 celery stalk, coarsely chopped
- Freshly ground black pepper
- 2 cups red wine
- 2 cups low-sodium beef broth
- 10 fresh thyme sprigs
- 2 bay leaves

DIRECTIONS

Step 1

Dry-brine the beef overnight (see Prepping Techniques).

Step 2

The next day, remove the beef from the refrigerator and pat dry with paper towels.

Step 3

Preheat the oven to 350°F.

Step 4

In a large, oven-safe pot, heat the oil over medium-high heat.

Step 5

Add the beef in a single layer. Cook for 8 to 12 minutes, turning every 2 to 3 minutes, or until browned on all sides. Transfer to a plate.

Step 6

Add the onion, carrot, and celery. Cook for 8 to 10 minutes, or until softened. Season with salt and pepper.

Step 7

Pour in the wine and broth to deglaze: Bring to a boil, and gently scrape the bottom of the pot with a wooden spoon to loosen any browned bits.

Step 8

Add the thyme and bay leaves. Cook for 13 to 15 minutes, or until the liquid is reduced by half, then add the beef. Cover the pot with a tight-fitting lid.

Step 9

Transfer the pot to the oven. Cook for 2½ to 2¾ hours, or until the beef is fork-tender. Remove from the oven. Rest for 20 minutes before serving.

Grilled Korean Short Ribs

COOKING METHOD: grill

SERVES: 4

PREP TIME: 15 minutes, plus at least 6 hours to marinate

COOK TIME: 10 to 15 minutes

INGREDIENTS

- ½ cup soy sauce
- ½ cup water
- ¼ cup sugar
- 2 tablespoons honey
- ¼ cup mirin
- 2 tablespoons sesame oil
- ½ Asian pear or any apple, grated
- ½ medium onion, grated
- 3 scallions, green and white parts, thinly sliced
- 2 tablespoons minced garlic
- 1 teaspoon minced fresh ginger
- ½ teaspoon freshly ground black pepper
- 1 teaspoon sesame seeds (optional)
- 3 pounds flanken-style short ribs (about ⅓ inch thick)

DIRECTIONS

Step 1

In a large nonreactive container, mix together the soy sauce, water, sugar, honey, mirin, sesame oil, pear, onion, scallions, garlic, ginger, pepper, and sesame seeds (if using).

Step 2

Put the short ribs in the marinade and refrigerate for 6 to 8 hours (overnight for best results).

Step 3

The next day, prepare the grill for direct grilling at 500°F.

Step 4

Remove the short ribs from the marinade, allowing any excess marinade to drip off.

Step 5

Grill the short ribs, turning once, for 2 to 3 minutes per side, or to your desired degree of doneness. Remove from the heat.

Grilled Skirt Steak with Salsa Criolla

COOKING METHOD: grill

SERVES: 8

PREP TIME: 5 minutes, plus overnight to dry-brine

COOK TIME: 5 minutes

INGREDIENTS

- 2½ pounds skirt steak
- Kosher salt, for dry-brining
- Vegetable oil, for coating the grill
- Freshly ground black pepper
- 1 batch Uruguayan Salsa Criolla

DIRECTIONS

Step 1

Dry-brine the beef overnight (see Prepping Techniques).

Step 2

The next day, remove the beef from the refrigerator and pat dry with paper towels.

Step 3

Prepare the grill for direct grilling at 650°F.

Step 4

Lightly coat the grill with oil.

Step 5

Put the steak on the grate and close the lid. Cook for 1 minute per side for medium rare. Remove from the heat. Season with pepper.

Step 6

Rest the steak for 5 minutes before slicing thinly across the grain at a 45-degree angle. Serve with the salsa.

Thai Grilled Beef Salad

COOKING METHOD: stovetop, grill

SERVES: 4

PREP TIME: 15 minutes, plus 2 hours to marinate

COOK TIME: 10 minutes

INGREDIENTS

- 1 pound skirt steak
- ¼ cup soy sauce
- ¼ cup sticky, jasmine, or long-grain rice
- Vegetable oil, for coating the grill
- 1 cup water
- ¼ cup beef broth
- 4 teaspoons sugar
- ¼ cup fish sauce
- Juice of 2 limes
- 1 tablespoon chili powder
- 1 tablespoon red pepper flakes
- 4 shallots, very thinly sliced
- 4 scallions, white and green parts, cut into thin rounds
- 1⅓ cups fresh mint leaves
- 8 culantro leaves (aka sawtooth herb) or ½ cup thinly sliced escarole or dandelion greens
- Steamed sticky rice or jasmine rice, for serving

DIRECTIONS

Step 1

Place the steak and soy sauce in a nonreactive container. Refrigerate, and marinate the steak for 2 hours.

Step 2

Heat a small skillet over medium heat until warm.

Step 3

Add the rice. Cook, shaking occasionally, for 3 to 4 minutes, or until toasted. Remove from the heat. Transfer to a plate. Let cool completely.

Step 4

Transfer the toasted rice to a spice grinder. Grind until the consistency of fine sand but still a bit crunchy.

Step 5

Remove the steak from the refrigerator and pat dry with paper towels.

Step 6

Prepare the grill for direct grilling at 650°F.

Step 7

Lightly coat the grill with oil.

Step 8

Put the steak on the grate and close the lid. Cook for 1 minute per side for medium rare. Remove from the heat.

Step 9

Rest the steak for 5 minutes before slicing thinly across the grain at a 45-degree angle.

Step 10

In a small pot, bring the water and beef broth to a boil.

1DIRECTIONS

Step 1

Add the sugar and fish sauce. Once the sugar has dissolved, remove from the heat.

Step 12

Add the lime juice, chili powder, and red pepper flakes.

Step 13

In a mixing bowl, combine the dressing, shallots, beef, scallions, mint, culantro, and toasted rice powder. Mix well. Serve with steamed rice.

The Ultimate Steak Sauce

COOKING METHOD: stovetop

MAKES: ¾ cup

PREP TIME: 5 minutes

COOK TIME: 10 to 15 minutes

INGREDIENTS

- ¼ onion, cut into 4 wedges

- 3 prunes, coarsely chopped

- ¼ cup soy sauce

- ¼ cup water

- 2 tablespoons extra-virgin olive oil

- 1 tablespoon Worcestershire sauce

- 1 teaspoon onion powder

- ¼ teaspoon cayenne

DIRECTIONS

Step 1

Heat a small saucepan over high heat for about 5 minutes, or until smoking hot.

Step 2

Place the onion wedges in the pan. Cook, undisturbed, for 3 to 4 minutes, or until charred.

Step 3

Flip the onion wedges. Cook, undisturbed, for 3 to 4 minutes, or until charred.

Step 4

Remove from the heat. Transfer the onion wedges to a food processor.

Step 5

Add the prunes, soy sauce, water, oil, Worcestershire sauce, onion powder, and cayenne. Blend until mostly smooth, with a few chunks remaining. Let cool to room temperature before serving.

Chateaubriand Sauce

COOKING METHOD: stovetop

MAKES: 2 cups

PREP TIME: 20 minutes

COOK TIME: 1½ hours

INGREDIENTS

- 3 tablespoons unsalted butter, divided
- 1 thick-cut bacon slice, chopped
- 1 small onion, coarsely chopped
- 1 small carrot, coarsely chopped
- 1 tablespoon all-purpose flour
- 1 batch Bordelaise Sauce
- 2 cups low-sodium beef broth
- 1 small tomato, coarsely chopped
- 1 tablespoon tomato paste
- 1 garlic clove, peeled and crushed
- 1 fresh tarragon sprig
- 3 dried porcini mushrooms, soaked in warm water
- 4 ounces sliced white mushrooms
- 1 shallot, minced
- Kosher salt

- Freshly ground black pepper
- 3 tablespoons brandy

DIRECTIONS

Step 1

In a medium pan, melt 1 tablespoon of butter over medium heat.

Step 2

Add the bacon. Cook, stirring occasionally, for 3 to 4 minutes, or until lightly browned.

Step 3

Add the onion and carrot. Cook for 6 to 7 minutes, or until starting to brown.

Step 4

Stir in the flour, coating the vegetables. Cook, undisturbed, for 3 to 4 minutes, or until browned.

Step 5

Pour in the Bordelaise Sauce and beef broth and stir vigorously to eliminate lumps. Bring to a simmer.

Step 6

Add the tomato, tomato paste, garlic, and tarragon. Simmer for 1 hour, or until the flavors meld. Remove from the heat.

Step 7

Meanwhile, in another medium pan, melt the remaining 2 tablespoons of butter over medium heat.

Step 8

Strain the porcini mushrooms, reserving the liquid, and pat dry. Add the porcini and white mushrooms to the pan. Cook, stirring infrequently, for 10 to 12 minutes, or until golden brown.

Step 9

Reduce the heat to medium-low. Add the shallot, and cook for 1 to 2 minutes, or until softened but not browned. Season with salt and pepper.

Step 10

Off the heat, pour in the brandy. Increase the heat to high, put the pan back on the burner, and carefully tip it just enough to ignite the brandy.

1DIRECTIONS

Step 1

Once the flames have died down, add the sauce from the first pan and as much of the porcini-soaking liquid as you prefer (I like ½ cup).

Step 12

Reduce the heat to low. Cook for 15 minutes, or until the sauce coats the back of a spoon. Remove from the heat. Season with salt and pepper.

Bordelaise Sauce

COOKING METHOD: stovetop

MAKES: 1 cup

PREP TIME: 5 minutes

COOK TIME: 15 to 20 minutes

INGREDIENTS

- 1 tablespoon unsalted butter
- 1 shallot, minced
- ½ cup red wine
- ½ cup demi-glace
- Handful fresh thyme sprigs
- 1 bay leaf
- Kosher salt
- Freshly ground black pepper

DIRECTIONS

Step 1

In a small saucepan, melt the butter over medium-low heat without browning.

Step 2

Add the shallots. Cook, stirring occasionally, for 3 to 4 minutes, or until softened and translucent.

Step 3

Add the wine, demi-glace, thyme, and bay leaf. Increase the heat to high. Bring to a boil, then reduce the heat to a simmer. Cook for 7 to 9 minutes, or until the sauce coats the back of a spoon. Season with salt and pepper. Remove from the heat and discard the bay leaf and thyme. Serve immediately.

Béarnaise Sauce

COOKING METHOD: stovetop

MAKES: 1½ cups

PREP TIME: 5 minutes

COOK TIME: 15 minutes

INGREDIENTS

- ⅓ cup white wine vinegar
- 1 shallot, minced

- 1 teaspoon crushed black peppercorns
- 1 teaspoon dried tarragon
- 7 ounces ghee
- 2 large egg yolks
- ¾ cup water
- 1 teaspoon finely chopped fresh tarragon
- Kosher salt
- Freshly ground black pepper

DIRECTIONS

Step 1

In a small pot, combine the vinegar, shallot, crushed peppercorns, and dried tarragon. Bring to a simmer over medium heat. Cook for 2 to 3 minutes, or until reduced to about 2 tablespoons. Strain, discarding the solids.

Step 2

Set up a double boiler: Fill a medium pot with about 1 inch of water. Place a bowl on top that fits snugly without touching the water. Bring the water to a simmer over medium-high heat.

Step 3

Meanwhile, in a small pan, melt the ghee over low heat.

Step 4

In the double boiler, combine the egg yolks, water, and vinegar reduction. Whisk continuously for 7 to 9 minutes, or until the volume doubles.

Step 5

In a slow, steady stream, pour in the ghee while whisking continuously, slowly at first, then faster as the sauce starts to emulsify, or come together and thicken until it coats the back of a spoon.

Step 6

Add the fresh tarragon. Season with salt and pepper. Serve immediately.

Chimichurri

COOKING METHOD: none
 MAKES: ½ cup
PREP TIME: 5 minutes

INGREDIENTS

- 1 garlic clove
- 4 cups flat-leaf parsley leaves
- Juice of 2 lemons or ¼ cup red wine vinegar

- ¼ cup extra-virgin olive oil
- ¼ teaspoon red pepper flakes
- ½ teaspoon kosher salt

DIRECTIONS

Step 1

Put the garlic, parsley, lemon juice, oil, red pepper flakes, and salt in a small food processor. Blend until combined.

Step 2

Use immediately, or transfer to an airtight container and refrigerate for up to 3 days.

Mexican Salsa Verde

COOKING METHOD: none
 MAKES: about 1 cup
PREP TIME: 5 minutes

INGREDIENTS

- ¼ cup extra-virgin olive oil
- 4 ounces tomatillos, cored and coarsely chopped
- 3 cups fresh cilantro
- ¼ cup diced white onion
- 1 jalapeño, seeded, stemmed, and coarsely chopped
- 1 teaspoon kosher salt
- 1 teaspoon red pepper flakes
- Juice of ½ lime

DIRECTIONS

Step 1

In a food processor, combine the olive oil, tomatillos, cilantro, onion, jalapeño, salt, red pepper flakes, and lime juice. Blend thoroughly.

Step 2

Use immediately, or transfer to an airtight container and refrigerate for up to 5 days.

Carne Asada

COOKING METHOD: grill
SERVES: 4
PREP TIME: 5 minutes, plus 1 to 2 hours to marinate
COOK TIME: 5 minutes

INGREDIENTS

For the steak
- 1 pound skirt steak
- 1 batch Cristian's Carne Asada Marinade
- Vegetable oil, for coating the grill
- Freshly ground black pepper

For the tacos
- Corn tortillas, for serving
- 1 container store-bought guacamole, for serving
- Chopped white onions, for serving
- Chopped fresh cilantro, for serving
- 1 batch Mexican Salsa Verde , for serving

To make the steak
DIRECTIONS
Step 1
Place the steak and marinade in a nonreactive container. Refrigerate, and marinate the steak for 1 to 2 hours.
Step 2
Remove the steak from the refrigerator and pat dry with paper towels.
Step 3
Prepare the grill for direct grilling at 650°F.
Step 4
Lightly coat the grill with oil.
Step 5
Put the steak on the grate and close the lid. Cook for 1 minute per side for medium rare. Remove from the heat. Season with pepper.
Step 6
Rest the steak for 5 minutes before slicing thinly across the grain at a 45-degree angle.

To make the tacos
Step 7

If you'd like to make tacos, throw some tortillas on the grill while it's still hot, and heat until just pliable. Transfer to a plate. Wrap with a clean kitchen towel to keep warm.

Step 8

Serve the carne asada with the tortillas, guacamole, onions, cilantro, and salsa.

Beef and Barley Soup

COOKING METHOD: stovetop

SERVES: 6

PREP TIME: 10 minutes, plus overnight to dry-brine

COOK TIME: 2 to 2¼ hours

INGREDIENTS

- 1 (1¼-pound) beef shank
- Kosher salt, for dry-brining and seasoning
- 1 tablespoon vegetable oil
- 1 onion, coarsely chopped
- 2 carrots, coarsely chopped
- 2 celery stalks, coarsely chopped
- 3 garlic cloves, coarsely chopped
- Freshly ground black pepper
- 2 quarts beef broth
- 2 teaspoons onion powder
- 2 bay leaves
- ½ cup pearl barley

DIRECTIONS

Step 1

Dry-brine the beef overnight (see Prepping Techniques).

Step 2

The next day, remove the beef from the refrigerator and pat dry with paper towels.

Step 3

In a large pot, heat the oil over high heat.

Step 4

Add the beef. Cook for 3 to 4 minutes per side, or until browned. Transfer to a plate.

Step 5

Reduce the heat to medium. Add the onion, carrots, celery, and garlic. Cook, stirring occasionally, for 8 to 10 minutes, or until softened and browned. Season with salt and pepper.

Step 6

Pour in the broth to deglaze: Bring to a boil, and gently scrape the bottom of the pot with a wooden spoon to loosen any browned bits.

Step 7

Add the onion powder, bay leaves, and beef. Bring to a simmer. Reduce the heat to medium-low. Cover with a tight-fitting lid. Cook, stirring occasionally to make sure nothing sticks to the bottom of the pot, for 1½ to 1¾ hours, or until the beef is tender. In the last 20 minutes of cooking, stir in the barley. Remove from the heat.

Step 8

Using tongs, transfer the beef shank to a work surface. Once cool enough to handle, using two forks, pick the meat off the bone, and shred. Discard the bay leaves and return the meat to the pot.

Step 9

Season with salt and pepper. Serve immediately.

Braised Beef Shank with Root Vegetables

SERVES: 6

PREP TIME: 15 minutes, plus overnight to dry-brine

COOK TIME: 2½ to 3 hours

INGREDIENTS

- 1 (1¼-pound) beef shank
- Kosher salt, for dry-brining and seasoning
- 1 tablespoon vegetable oil
- 2 tablespoons unsalted butter
- 1 onion, coarsely chopped
- 2 carrots, coarsely chopped
- 2 celery stalks, coarsely chopped
- 3 garlic cloves, coarsely chopped
- Freshly ground black pepper
- 2 tablespoons tomato paste
- 1 cup red wine (optional)
- 3 cups beef broth (4 cups if not using wine)
- 2 or 3 fresh rosemary sprigs
- 2 bay leaves

- 1 celeriac, peeled and cut into large chunks

- 1 large turnip, peeled and cut into large chunks

- 1 rutabaga, peeled and cut into large chunks

DIRECTIONS

Step 1

Dry-brine the beef overnight (see Prepping Techniques).

Step 2

The next day, remove the beef from the refrigerator and pat dry with paper towels.

Step 3

Preheat the oven to 350°F.

Step 4

In a large, oven-safe pot, heat the oil over high heat.

Step 5

Add the beef. Cook for 3 to 4 minutes per side, or until browned on all sides. Transfer to a plate.

Step 6

Reduce the heat to medium. Melt the butter. Add the onion, carrots, celery, and garlic. Cook, stirring occasionally, for 8 to 10 minutes, or until softened and browned. Season with salt and pepper.

Step 7

Add the tomato paste. Cook for 1 minute, or until bright red.

Step 8

Pour in the wine (if using) and beef broth to deglaze: Increase the heat to high. Bring to a boil, and gently scrape the bottom of the pot with a wooden spoon to loosen any browned bits.

Step 9

Add the beef, rosemary, bay leaves, celeriac, turnip, and rutabaga. Cover the pot with a tight-fitting lid.

Step 10

Transfer the pot to the oven. Cook for 2 to 2½ hours, or until the beef is tender. Remove from the oven. Discard the bay leaves. Skim off any excess fat. Serve immediately.

Texas Barbecued Beef Brisket

COOKING METHOD: smoker

SERVES: 10 to 12

PREP TIME: 15 to 30 minutes, plus overnight to dry-brine

COOK TIME: 7½ to 9½ hours, plus resting 1 to 2 hours

INGREDIENTS

- 1 (8- to 10-pound) whole packer beef brisket

- Kosher salt, for dry-brining
- 3 tablespoons freshly ground black pepper

DIRECTIONS

Step 1

Trim the fat cap of the brisket to ¼-inch thickness. Remove any hard fat. Square off the edges: Trim all the sides to make straight lines along the edges for even cooking.

Step 2

Dry-brine the brisket overnight (see Prepping Techniques).

Step 3

The next day, remove the brisket from the refrigerator. Season with the pepper. Soak wood chunks (preferably oak or pecan, but any nonresinous hardwood will do) for at least 15 minutes. Preheat the smoker to 250°F to 275°F, and add the soaked wood, following the manufacturer's instructions.

Step 4

Place the brisket on the grate over the drip pan, fat-side up, and close the lid. Add wood and fuel as needed to maintain smoke and temperature. Wrap the brisket in foil after 5 to 6 hours, or once the bark is dark brown. Avoid opening the lid unnecessarily; this will prolong the cook time significantly.

Step 5

Turn over the brisket, and cook for 2½ to 3½ hours, or until an instant-read thermometer inserted into the center registers 200°F. Remove from the smoker.

Step 6

Rest the brisket, wrapped in foil, for 1 to 2 hours before serving. Cut across the grain into ¼-inch-thick slices.

Argentine Grilled Flank Steak

COOKING METHOD: grill
SERVES: 8
PREP TIME: 5 minutes, plus overnight to dry-brine
COOK TIME: 5 to 10 minutes

INGREDIENTS

- 1 (2½-pound) flank steak
- Kosher salt, for dry-brining
- Vegetable oil, for coating the grill
- Freshly ground black pepper
- ½ cup Chimichurri

DIRECTIONS

Step 1

Dry-brine the steak overnight (see Prepping Techniques).

Step 2

The next day, remove the steak from the refrigerator and pat dry with paper towels.

Step 3

Prepare the grill for direct grilling at 650°F.

Step 4

Lightly coat the grill with oil.

Step 5

Put the steak on the grate and close the lid. Cook for 2½ to 3 minutes per side for medium, or until an instant-read thermometer inserted into the side registers 130°F. Remove from the heat. Season with pepper.

Step 6

Rest the steak for 5 minutes before slicing thinly across the grain at a 45-degree angle. Serve with the chimichurri.

Aioli

COOKING METHOD: none

 MAKES: 1¼ cups

PREP TIME: 5 minutes

INGREDIENTS

- 1 large egg (preferably pasteurized)
- 1 cup vegetable oil
- 2 garlic cloves
- ½ teaspoon kosher salt

DIRECTIONS

Step 1

Place the egg in a small food processor. Blend until beaten.

Step 2

With the machine running, slowly stream in the oil until emulsified.

Step 3

Blend in the garlic and salt.

Step 4

Use immediately, or transfer to an airtight container and refrigerate for up to 5 days.

Horseradish Sauce

COOKING METHOD: stovetop

 MAKES: about 1 cup

PREP TIME: 10 minutes

COOK TIME: 10 minutes

INGREDIENTS

- 1 tablespoon unsalted butter
- 1 shallot, minced
- 1 cup heavy cream
- 2 tablespoons freshly grated horseradish
- 1 tablespoon Dijon mustard
- 1 bay leaf
- Kosher salt
- Freshly ground black pepper

DIRECTIONS

Step 1

In a small saucepan, melt the butter over medium-low heat.

Step 2

Add the shallot. Cook for 1 to 2 minutes, or until softened.

Step 3

Add the cream, horseradish, mustard, and bay leaf. Season with salt and pepper. Increase the heat to medium. Bring to a simmer. Cook for 5 to 6 minutes, or until the sauce coats the back of a spoon. Remove from the heat. Remove and discard the bay leaf. Serve immediately.

Step 4

Store any leftover Horseradish Sauce in an airtight container in the refrigerator for up to 3 days.

Uruguayan Salsa Criolla

COOKING METHOD: none

 MAKES: about 1½ cups

PREP TIME: 5 minutes

INGREDIENTS

- ½ cup diced tomatoes
- ½ cup diced green bell pepper
- ¼ cup diced red onion

- 2 tablespoons extra-virgin olive oil
- ¼ cup red wine vinegar
- 2 tablespoons chopped fresh oregano
- 8 garlic cloves, minced
- Juice of ½ lime
- Kosher salt
- Freshly ground black pepper

DIRECTIONS

Step 1

In a bowl, mix together the tomatoes, bell pepper, onion, oil, vinegar, oregano, garlic, and lime juice. Season with salt and pepper.

Cristian's Carne Asada Marinade

COOKING METHOD: none

 MAKES: about 1 cup

PREP TIME: 5 minutes

INGREDIENTS

- ½ cup vegetable oil
- 2½ tablespoons kosher salt
- 1 tablespoon dried oregano, preferably Mexican
- 1 head garlic, peeled
- 1 jalapeño, stemmed
- Stems from 1 bunch cilantro
- Juice of 1 orange
- Juice of 1 lime
- 1 tablespoon soy sauce

DIRECTIONS

Step 1

In a food processor, combine the oil, salt, oregano, garlic, jalapeño, cilantro stems, orange juice, lime juice, and soy sauce. Blend thoroughly.

Step 2

Use immediately, or transfer to an airtight container and refrigerate for up to 5 days.

Roasted Potatoes

COOKING METHOD: oven
SERVES: 4
PREP TIME: 5 minutes
COOK TIME: 30 to 35 minutes

INGREDIENTS

- 1½ pounds baby creamer potatoes, halved (quartered if large)
- 2 teaspoons vegetable oil
- Kosher salt
- Freshly ground black pepper
- 2 tablespoons chopped fresh herbs, such as thyme, rosemary, or parsley

DIRECTIONS

Step 1

Preheat the oven to 475°F.

Step 2

In a large bowl, toss the potatoes with the oil. Season with salt. Transfer to a sheet pan in a single layer.

Step 3

Transfer the sheet pan to the oven. Roast, tossing once, for 30 to 35 minutes, or until golden brown and crisp around the edges. Remove from the oven. Season with pepper. Sprinkle with the herbs. Serve immediately.

Mashed Potatoes

COOKING METHOD: stovetop
SERVES: 4
PREP TIME: 5 minutes
COOK TIME: 20 minutes

INGREDIENTS

- 1½ pounds baby creamer potatoes, halved (quartered if large)
- Kosher salt
- 8 tablespoons (1 stick) unsalted butter
- ½ cup heavy cream, gently warmed
- Freshly ground black pepper
- 1 scallion, green and white parts, finely chopped

DIRECTIONS

Step 1

In a medium pot, cover the potatoes by 1 inch of heavily salted, cold water. Bring to a simmer over high heat. Reduce the heat to maintain the simmer. Cook for 10 to 12 minutes, or until easily pierced with a fork. Drain.

Step 2

Return the potatoes to the pot over medium heat. Cook, shaking occasionally, for about 3 minutes so any remaining moisture evaporates. Remove from the heat. Transfer to a bowl.

Step 3

Add the butter and cream. Using a fork or a potato masher, mash to your desired consistency. Season with pepper.

Step 4

Add the scallion. Serve immediately.

Grilled Asparagus

COOKING METHOD: grill
SERVES: 4
PREP TIME: 5 minutes
COOK TIME: 5 minutes

INGREDIENTS

- 2 pounds asparagus, woody ends trimmed
- 1 tablespoon extra-virgin olive oil
- 1 tablespoon vegetable oil
- Kosher salt
- Freshly ground black pepper

DIRECTIONS

Step 1

Prepare the grill for direct grilling at 500°F.

Step 2

In a large bowl, toss the asparagus with the olive oil and vegetable oil. Season with salt.

Step 3

Put the asparagus on the grate and close the lid. Cook, turning once, for 1 to 2 minutes, or until crisp-tender and charred. Transfer to a serving dish. Season with pepper. Serve immediately.

Roasted Brussels Sprouts

COOKING METHOD: oven
SERVES: 4
PREP TIME: 5 minutes
COOK TIME: 15 minutes

INGREDIENTS

- 1 pound Brussels sprouts, halved
- 1 tablespoon vegetable oil
- Kosher salt
- Freshly ground black pepper
- Zest of 1 lemon

DIRECTIONS

Step 1

Preheat the oven to 450°F.

Step 2

In a large bowl, toss the Brussels sprouts with the oil. Season with salt. Transfer to a sheet pan in a single layer.

Step 3

Transfer the sheet pan to the oven. Roast for 12 to 15 minutes, or until tender and lightly charred in spots. Remove from the oven. Season with pepper. Sprinkle with the lemon zest. Serve immediately.

Grilled Corn

COOKING METHOD: grill
SERVES: 4
PREP TIME: 5 minutes
COOK TIME: 20 to 25 minutes

INGREDIENTS

- 4 ears corn, husked
- 2 teaspoons vegetable oil
- Kosher salt
- 2 tablespoons unsalted butter

DIRECTIONS

Step 1

Prepare the grill for direct grilling at 500°F.

Step 2

In a large bowl, toss the corn with the oil. Season with salt.

Step 3

Put the corn on the grate and close the lid. Cook, turning one quarter turn every 5 to 6 minutes, for 20 to 25 minutes, or until tender and charred. Transfer to a serving dish. Top each cob with butter. Serve immediately.

Lobster Mac 'n' Cheese

SERVES: 6
PREP TIME: 15 minutes
COOK TIME: 45 minutes
INGREDIENTS

- Kosher salt

- 1 lobster tail

- 2½ cups dried macaroni

- 3 cups milk

- 4 tablespoons (½ stick) unsalted butter

- 5 tablespoons all-purpose flour

- Pinch cayenne

- 1 teaspoon freshly ground white pepper

- 12 ounces Gruyère, grated

- 1 cup seasoned bread crumbs

DIRECTIONS

Step 1

Preheat the oven to 350°F.

Step 2

In a large pot, bring water to a gentle boil and salt it until it tastes like the sea.

Step 3

Prepare an ice bath by filling a small bowl with ice water.

Step 4

Using a pair of kitchen shears, cut down the center of the underside of the lobster tail. Spread the shell to expose the meat. Add the lobster to the water. Cook for 1 minute per ounce, or until the shell is bright red and the meat separates easily from the shell.

Step 5

Using tongs, plunge the lobster into the ice bath. Once it is cool enough to handle, remove the meat from the shell and chop.

Step 6

Return the water to a boil. Add the macaroni. Cook for 5 minutes, or until al dente, and drain.

Step 7

In a small saucepan, heat the milk over medium heat just until it comes to a simmer. Turn off the heat, and cover with a lid to keep warm.

Step 8

Meanwhile, in a large, oven-safe skillet, melt the butter over medium heat until the foam subsides.

Step 9

Add the flour and whisk continuously, making sure no lumps form, for 3 to 5 minutes, or until the mixture is light brown.

Step 10

Add the milk and bring to a boil. Watch to make sure it does not boil over.

Step 11

When it comes to a boil, reduce the heat to a simmer and whisk continuously until the sauce coats the back of a spoon.

Step 12

Season with 1 teaspoon of salt and the cayenne and the white pepper. Stir in the macaroni, lobster, and cheese.

Step 13

Top with the bread crumbs and transfer to the oven. Bake for 15 to 20 minutes, or until the top browns. Remove from the oven. Serve immediately.

Caesar Salad

COOKING METHOD: oven
SERVES: 6
PREP TIME: 20 minutes
COOK TIME: 15 minutes
INGREDIENTS

For the croutons
- 4 cups torn baguette pieces
- 2 tablespoons extra-virgin olive oil
- Kosher salt
- Freshly ground black pepper

For the salad

- 6 anchovy fillets
- 6 garlic cloves, peeled
- Kosher salt
- 2 large egg yolks
- ¼ cup freshly squeezed lemon juice
- ½ cup extra-virgin olive oil
- 1 tablespoon smooth Dijon mustard
- 1 teaspoon Worcestershire sauce
- ½ cup finely grated Parmigiano-Reggiano, plus more for shaving
- Freshly ground black pepper
- 3 romaine hearts, leaves separated and left whole

To make the croutons

DIRECTIONS

Step 1

Preheat the oven to 350°F.

Step 2

In a bowl, toss the baguette pieces with the olive oil, salt, and pepper.

Step 3

Spread the baguette pieces out in a single layer on a sheet pan. Transfer the sheet pan to the oven. Toast for 12 to 15 minutes, or until golden brown. Remove from the oven. The croutons can be made up to 1 day ahead.

To make the salad

Step 4

Finely chop the anchovies and garlic together with a pinch of salt. Using the side of your knife, mash into a paste. Transfer to a large bowl.

Step 5

Add the egg yolks and lemon juice. Whisk together while slowly streaming in the olive oil to form an emulsion.

Step 6

Stir in the mustard, Worcestershire sauce, and cheese. Season with salt and pepper.

Step 7

Add the romaine and croutons. Toss with your hands until well incorporated. Season with salt and plenty of pepper. Shave more cheese over the salad. Serve immediately.

AYCE KBBQ Salad

COOKING METHOD: none
SERVES: 6
PREP TIME: 20 minutes

INGREDIENTS

- 2 tablespoons rice vinegar
- 2 tablespoons vegetable oil
- 1 teaspoon toasted sesame oil
- 1 teaspoon soy sauce
- 1 teaspoon sugar
- 1 teaspoon grated fresh ginger
- Kosher salt
- 10 ounces romaine lettuce, thinly sliced
- 4 scallions, green and white parts, thinly sliced on a bias
- Freshly ground black pepper

DIRECTIONS

Step 1

In a large bowl, whisk together the vinegar, vegetable oil, sesame oil, soy sauce, sugar, and ginger until the sugar has dissolved. Season with salt.

Step 2

Add the lettuce and scallions. Toss to combine. Season with salt and pepper. Serve immediately.

Tabbouleh

COOKING METHOD: stovetop
SERVES: 6
PREP TIME: 20 minutes
COOK TIME: 15 minutes

INGREDIENTS

- ½ cup medium bulgur wheat
- ¾ cup water
- 3 cups finely chopped flat-leaf parsley (from about 4 bunches)
- 1 pint grape tomatoes, finely diced
- 1 cup seeded and finely diced cucumber

- ¼ cup finely diced red onion
- ¼ cup extra-virgin olive oil
- Juice of 2 lemons
- Kosher salt
- Freshly ground black pepper

DIRECTIONS

Step 1

In a small pot, combine the bulgur and water. Bring to a simmer. Reduce the heat to the lowest possible, and cover with a tight-fitting lid. Cook for about 12 minutes, or until tender. Remove from the heat. Let stand for 10 minutes, then transfer to a large bowl and refrigerate until cool.

Step 2

Add the parsley, tomatoes, cucumber, onion, oil, and lemon juice. Season with salt and pepper. Serve immediately.

Green Beans Almondine

SERVES: 4
PREP TIME: 5 minutes
COOK TIME: 20 minutes
INGREDIENTS

For the almonds
- ½ cup slivered almonds

For the green beans
- 4 quarts water
- ½ cup Diamond Crystal kosher salt or ¼ cup Morton's kosher salt, plus more for seasoning
- 1 pound haricots verts, trimmed
- 1 tablespoon unsalted butter
- 3 garlic cloves, chopped
- Freshly ground black pepper

To make the almonds
DIRECTIONS
Step 1

Preheat the oven to 350°F.

Step 2

Spread the almonds out in a single layer on a sheet pan. Transfer the sheet pan to the oven. Toast for 14 to 16 minutes, or until golden brown. Remove from the oven. The almonds can be toasted up to 2 days ahead.

To make the green beans

Step 3

In a large pot, bring the water and salt to a boil.

Step 4

Add the haricots verts. Cook for 3 minutes, or until bright green and crisp-tender. Drain.

Step 5

In a large skillet, melt the butter over medium heat.

Step 6

Add the garlic. Cook for 1 to 2 minutes, or until fragrant.

Step 7

Add the haricots verts and almonds. Toss to combine. Season with salt and pepper. Cook, stirring, for 1 to 2 minutes, or until the flavors have melded. Remove from the heat. Serve immediately.

Perfect French Fries

COOKING METHOD: stovetop
SERVES: 4
PREP TIME: 20 minutes
COOK TIME: 30 minutes
INGREDIENTS

- 1 quart vegetable oil
- 2 pounds russet potatoes
- Kosher salt
- Freshly ground black pepper

DIRECTIONS

Step 1

In a 3-quart pot, heat the oil to 300°F.

Step 2

Peel the potatoes and cut into ¼-inch matchsticks. Transfer to a bowl of cold water.

Step 3

When ready to fry, lift the potatoes out of the water and transfer to a clean kitchen towel. Wring them dry.

Step 4

Fry, in batches if necessary to prevent overcrowding, for 2 to 3 minutes, or until the fries float to the top (they should not brown). Increase the heat as needed to maintain temperature. Put cooked fries on a paper-towel-lined plate and allow the oil to return to temperature between batches.

Step 5

When all the potatoes have been blanched, increase the oil temperature to 350°F.

Step 6

Fry again, in batches if necessary, for 5 to 6 minutes, or until crisp and browned. Adjust the heat as needed to maintain temperature. Allow the oil to return to temperature between batches. Drain on paper towels. Season each batch with salt and pepper immediately.

Printed in Great Britain
by Amazon